I0843442

MOSTLY FAKE

**Illustrations and Theory
by Karen Kellock Ph.D.**

This is a new theory in psychology. According to Koestler, all landmark theories are presented in picture-strip format (right-left integration) to bring on the "aha" experience of the formula (the characteristic of all new paradigms).

FORMULA FOR THEORY:

**ALL SUCCESS ATTRACTION
ALL DISEASE OBSTRUCTION
ALL RECOVERY ELIMINATION**

**The three obstructions are:
people, habit and food.**

**Remove your obstruction and
you snap to your goals,
waiting in the wings.**

MOSTLY FAKE

Instead of hungering for his attention you finally had enough of one-way conversation. When you've had enough it happens in a blink of an eye: freedom from a nut. You have no mind of your own that's clearly shown by acceptance of whatever comes along. Arrogant stiff-necked grin, you see it in liberal friends. They act so superior we cave in to fear. They know they're right but are so wrong it's clear.

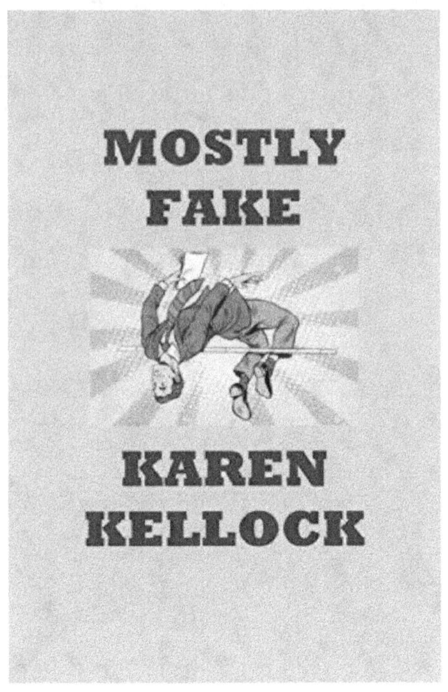

MOSTLY FAKE

YOU'VE HAD ENOUGH OF NOTHING
YOU'RE WASTING YOUR TIME
KNOW YOUR VALUES AND WANTS
DON'T BE A BOOTIE CALL
MISTRESS IS THE LOWEST
HOME NOT A ROLL IN THE HAY
NEEDING CONNECTION GOES WRONG
WE'VE BEEN IGNORED
GOSSIP DISAPPEARS
HE DON'T WANT YOU
MEN WANNA BREAK HER DOWN
DEEP THROAT
PUSHOVERS AREN'T RESPECTED
HE CAME BACK OUTA EGO
BUSTING BUBBLES ABOUT PEOPLE
MAKING GOLD AND FORGIVENESS
MAKE GOLD ON RESENTMENTS
SOCIAL DEVICES ARE A TURN OFF
SEE FOES AS A GIFT
EASY WOMEN
TWO ENDS AND ONE IS VERY BAD
SOCIAL MATRIX OR IT'S ILLNESS
JESUS WAS SPECIFIC ON HELL
HOMOSEXUAL SIN: A LITMUS TEST
NORMALIZING PERVERSION
GAYS AREN'T NICE
LIBERAL ELITES AREN'T NICE
A WRITER WRITES WITHOUT STOP
TURN OFF THE ENDLESS SPOUT
EMOTIONAL CUTOFF VS. PERSISTENT SYMPTOMS
THE KAREN KELLOCK PICTURESTRIP

FORWARD TO PROJECTION VICTIMS

We're not in competition in our own stream. It's not like if I get more you get less. It's infinite.

The hedge was down so I could see what I should want. In came evil so I wanted only love.

Just like the hedge is down for America so we see what we should want. It's Trump not chumps.

DEALING WITH NEGATIVE PROJECTIONS

I left off one association after another and escaped all evil talk. William James on the saints.

People don't know you and project onto you so if you don't stand up you'll be broken in two.

It was hard to deal with negative projections of others who didn't even know me--bummer.

If someone is empty/has no identity he's a sponge to bad projections until he knows "me".

If they haven't learned to deal with their own negative emotions they'll project em onto you son.

All relationships are projections which allow us to see what's going on inside. Jenna Ryan

FIGHTING SLANDER WITHOUT A SELF

Without a self, when confronted with false projections we internalize it as true and ACT IT OUT.

Swallowing [introjecting] negative projections brings compensations to deny the accusations.

Negative projections are horrible but a simple boundary can prevent any more trouble.

Forward to Projection Victims

All will take advantage. Even the sweetest will gain power if you allow a boundary to relax.

MADDENING MISJUDGMENT

They came at me accusatorially and it was like they owned me. I felt possessed and lonely.

If I reacted [stunned] with anger it proved them right. How we react is crucial at this point.

I would try to disprove them, throwing me outa grace. In reacting to them I wasn't the Ace.

I'd try to be like Jesus who did not defend Himself. This was a hard life, an emotional hell.

Get outa there, go grey rock, go back to people who love you and who are human, amen.

There is no greater loneliness than to be so misjudged without being self-aware enough.

I internalized their negative projections for decades and acted out their evil narratives.

NEVER AGAIN, LEARN YOUR LESSON

All you know is you never see that person again unchaperoned--protected from below.

I felt hopeless [stamped & bloodied by their projections] since it came from being dumb.

Even if I could explain myself they wouldn't have understood it--I cried out for God's help.

It felt like the witchcraft trials but it came from liberals! They were the worst accusers of all.

MOSTLY FAKE

YOU'VE HAD ENOUGH OF NOTHING

Instead of hungering for his attention you finally have had enough of one-way conversation.

You FINALLY have had enough and it all happens in a blink of an eye: freedom from a nut.

All I know is you go along with this crap no matter how much it changes and goes zigzag.

You have no mind of your own that's clearly shown by acceptance of whatever comes along.

Who are the liberal elite? Comics, mayors--anyone in the limelight: plastic surgery wins the fight.

Arrogant stiff-necked grin, arrogance being Satan's other name--you see it in liberal friends.

They act so superior we cave in to fear. They know they're right but are so wrong dear.

Lord puts one up as He puts another down. Success comes not from East or West but God.

With any sin God gives them up to a reprobate mind--a confused, crooked mind that's blind.

He lacks self so becomes a chameleon, an actor but he also CAVES IN when not being adored.

I have given up on one-way conversations cuz you can't relate/don't want to, whatever man.

MOSTLY FAKE

So he doesn't want to hear about you and he can't go deep--what do you see in this creep?

Unless a man gets to the heart of the matter he's boring to me cuz he's unsure or whatever.

You gotta go by the book not what society says. The blind leading the blind even your aunts.

When as a child you're ignored & disrespected the perception of the self is corrupted instead.

Mansell was de-chaired believing in Conversion Therapy cuz they're BORN THAT WAY.

YOU'RE WASTING YOUR TIME

You have psychological damage if you don't realize what's happening with silent treatment.

Narcissists live for attention and when they don't get it it's narcissistic injury and revenge soon.

His words don't match his actions. He says he cares but he mocks you in front of friends.

He said how empathic he was but I saw how demanding he was with the waiter.

Liberals are always labeling themselves good and kind but you see the opposite behavior, aye.

So he loves attention and his words don't match his actions: you're in a psych op whirlwind.

Things are always fine at first but soon you notice a callousness like standing you up.

MOSTLY FAKE

You're a sad sack: You feel like you're always chasing them but that energy never comes back.

This is where you check your boundaries. How much energy goes out vs. comes back honey?

She chased men always hoping they'd call her back. What a sad place to be in: avoid this crap.

KNOW YOUR VALUES AND WANTS

Always chasing with the mind map on default that she wasn't worthy and needed him surely.

She watched mom's reactions then downloaded her fear of men and stuffing her feelings then.

Don't waste your precious time! Some men like being chased cuz that's the power game, aye.

Invest your precious time to a committed relationship and withdraw energy/stop wasting it.

See the signs that you're wasting your time and a whole new life opens up in the light.

Notice he has totally different relationship goals and values. It's black and white you know.

Instead of arguing and hurting just notice the fact you have different goals & values, that's that.

DON'T BE A BOOTIE CALL

Don't ever settle for being a bootie call hoping things will work out later. Get a grip daughter.

She knew he wasn't that into her but hoped she could change this by having sex: RIDICULOUS.

MOSTLY FAKE

She thinks sex will make him fall in love with her tho' he never wants to take her out to dinner.

She thinks sex will make him love her when he'll never introduce her to his friends/family/mother.

If someone calls you for a bootie call you're wasting your time. Get that through your brain.

Our goal should be to increase self-awareness and this comes from detaching emotionally sis.

Major red flag: He calls you for bootie calls at midnight but you're never included in his real life.

Girl, you're settling just for what's showing up. Don't you dare do this daughter, love yourself.

If a man wants to come over for sex and that's it: lock him out, change number, call the cops.

For there is nothing so demeaning as to wake up the next morning after being used darling.

MISTRESS IS THE LOWEST

Face it and save yourself twit: This may not be what you want and it's a one-sided relationship.

Don't be strung along with a cad ["I'll leave my wife"] with no intentions of doing so: live right.

CAUTION: He may be just another narcissist or only interested in casual sex here & now.

If any man has the gall and audacity to come over just for sex he's your enemy as such witch.

More often than not the mistress is a marriage-maker not a breaker--you're enriching a traitor.

MOSTLY FAKE

Don't be the worst fool ever by being strung along for years. Life is a breath/soon it's over.

Who in the hell is just available for bootie calls but with emergency the guy's nowhere around?

Don't be a dam fool and see the **WHOLE PICTURE** not your instincts perverted by this lecher.

For sex--the birds and the bees--is a most powerful force intended to maintain the human race.

Don't allow the combo of sex and attachment trauma to bind you to a clown, a loser, a comet.

HOME NOT A ROLL IN THE HAY

You're a grown adult woman. If casual sex is all you want fine but you're out of your mind.

I want a man I can create a home for, love to his death and spoil every day not a roll in the hay.

You want a relationship, a marriage, a union for the long haul, a family, a household, love.

You want a man to put you behind a locked fence to love and spoil you to death: **BLESSED!**

As an adult it's his right if that's what he wants--bootie calls that's all--but you wanna walk tall.

Don't go for fake love, this is how you tell: are you dined in front of the world or hidden girl?

If you think this is all you deserve then that's all that's gonna show up. Queenology or rust/bust.

Setting boundaries is crucial so even if tempted you know what you ultimately want girl.

MOSTLY FAKE

No self-respecting woman would settle for bootie calls forgetting everything else she wants.

The "universe" delivers to you what you believe in so without self-lovin' that's all you're gettin'.

It's not the fault of the guy when you're available in a minute but respect: you're not gettin' it.

NEEDING CONNECTION GOES WRONG

You want connection so you adapt to him while ignoring your gut instincts--a SIREN.

Don't delude yourself in your loneliness that it's anything but a bootie call: keep this central.

Don't be taken in when he flatters/lovebombs but work it through to afterwards when he's gone.

You're the loser, genders aren't the same. You need commitment, that's how you're made.

Don't delude yourself in loneliness/his horniness that things will change/you won't be a mistress.

Love Addict: Every time you're used by him you must start a no-contact process all over again.

Don't be used again cuz the post-organismic withdrawal {POW] is so demeaning and brutal.

WE'VE BEEN IGNORED

The ignored [disconfirmed] thinks: does anyone even know I exist? Solution: transcend all this.

Main female device: to make you feel you don't exist, to ignore you to cut you down to size.

MOSTLY FAKE

For they are just the peanut gallery, the majority, the herd, the common narrative of the day ok.

Being ignored is a slap in the face especially knowing that's how they cut you down to size.

Hugging and kissing like monkey see monkey do. I'd do anything to escape the human zoo.

They are social fascists. And when you've been pegged it evokes all their mean hatreds.

I don't know who's worse, men or the women. Both are mean social fascists given the situation.

Since the feminist entry we're all abandoned babies with addictive crutches/an inner scream

When women aren't women they're harridans and everyone's scared of em, admit it man.

GOSSIP DISAPPEARS

Don't you worry about it--it's just something they heard. They meet you, it all disappears.

It's not a male thing to thrash around in bed with strangers one after another, some go higher.

By you blabbing all your business right off he knows just how to act to fit you like a glove.

The male thing starting relationship is to break her down not build her up unless he's like God.

Break her down, game her/put her thru the ringer. Take her dog, don't answer calls, tame her.

Break her down, keep her on her toes by keeping her confused, make her wonder about you.

MOSTLY FAKE

He wants you to pay for your sins. He doesn't want you to be forgiven but rub your nose in it.

Is he truly loving or insecure, weak, egoistic, immature, hurting, misguided and poorly raised?

HE DON'T WANT YOU

HE DON'T WANT YOU. These words replace all relationship therapy and begging too.

It's disgusting how females are chasing men. Stop it, stop it I beseech you common women.

When he explained the difference between liberal and conservative I saw everything different.

Living in la-la land utopia or hard facts correctly adapting: I saw the two maps suddenly.

Stop talking about sex you bum! I don't wanna picture you thrashing around with some woman.

Let God choose your next mate, ok? You haven't done so well in that area/you've really paid.

You make yourself available and pledge your undying love. This is not the order from above.

If he came back out of ego you still feel abrasiveness, distrust, out of place insensitiveness.

He never changed he just wiggled his way back to resume his spot cuz life didn't work out.

He lulled you to sleep with buzz words but came back without doing the work of growing.

He gives you gifts or quality time but it's not true quality, he's not a lover but a deceiver.

MOSTLY FAKE

In this era of women-hate men feel **THEY'RE** the prize but God said a good wife's hard to find.

As the weaker sex we're to be respected and protected but no more, we're often degraded.

MEN WANNA BREAK HER DOWN

They exchange notes how to break us down. He dropped me in a strange city, so did his friend.

But when a man comes back outa **HEART** he will be truly repentant and not just for lent.

The minute he starts to break you down you gotta walk away gently cuz he may get violent sweetie.

I grew so afraid of men my husband had to handle me with kid gloves but I still respected him.

He's twice your size, don't let him in. He wants to cut you down to size, reject and block him.

But when your guy has **HEART** he will truly study the toxic situation and make a fresh start.

He never hit me but yelled and rose up as if he were going to. This is violence/made me blue.

He came back for the cozy home/being served with everything there, then taking over.

It's so boring this groupie thing you got going, this fireside chat with good ol' boy chaps.

Six months picnics, museums, movies, dinners then marriage. Not kissing/the whole package.

DEEP THROAT

MOSTLY FAKE

"But we didn't go all the way". But you degrade yourself MORE by the other thing ok?

Hey you Deep Throat: You've been so degraded and the little floozie doesn't even know it.

A peck on the lips, that's it. You don't give no man a release or you're a floozy and a twit.

Manipulation by guilt, coercion by fear. He came back from ego and you say no sex: careful dear.

Now if he come back and he talkin' good DON'T GIVE IN or we'll have to start all over again.

If you give into that deceiver you'll be so sorry afterwards with his post-orgasmic turn.

PUSHOVERS AREN'T RESPECTED

If she's a pushover he won't respect her, ever. Men need challenge to want to protect her.

Spend money, get her roses, more quality time than before and she'll give in and he knows it.

Spend money, get her roses. More quality time than before: she'll give in and he knows it.

He's not your husband/hasn't committed to you and he doesn't even like you. Get a grip shrew.

SEX is the whole thing to men. It's your only leverage woman: give in and become a vixen.

You give into his words like a love-starved girl and HE GOT YOU, a degraded unpaid whore.

A couple months and now he's back to his old ways. Condescending, arrogant and nasty.

MOSTLY FAKE

Immature, insecure, ignorant man you knew before reappears just cuz you opened that door.

HE CAME BACK OUTA EGO

He came back to play ya. The snake couldn't stand being rejected so came back to get ya.

If you don't give a man sexual favors he ain't gonna fake it for long, you'll see who he is sister.

Some men will marry on demand: having been raised by savages so they don't give a dam.

He wants to win--to avenge the rejection--so will do anything to make you lay down for him.

Gotta be careful girls, you are the weaker sex/need a man who protects, so caveat: NO SEX.

What just happened? I got pregnant by a cheater who's not my husband. Lady who gave in.

Thinking about your ex: He's your ex for a reason so don't forget that. --survivor of narcissism.

Coming back from ego he seeks to implant you then when pregnant he will cheat on you.

To keep and love a man you must be able to lose him and leave him for good. Tony Gaskins

If a man doesn't believe you'll leave him you will never have his heart: ethics/standards.

The man coming from ego will show his true colors cuz he can't fake that for long you know.

BUSTING BUBBLES ABOUT PEOPLE

MOSTLY FAKE

I'm so sorry to bust your bubble, here you thought he was back. But he's the same--fact?

RECAP: Do not slip up on the bed with a grown man who's a boy who came back outa ego.

One date with "the one" and now you're a relationship coach. He dumps you, you're toast.

I've made many sins and transgressions with no right to talk but when it comes to sex, don't.

The reason I can write ten hours a day about this is cuz I been there done that and what a mess.

There are just three main things men think about: sex, sex, and sex. Tony Gaskins

I know it's depressing but there is hope. God is real, what He has for you cannot be broke.

When you get on your back too fast [he's the judge of that] he'll instantly peg you and its bad.

Give in too fast and he's truly aghast. He dates one who's chaste and puts her in a higher caste.

MAKING GOLD AND FORGIVENESS

Refuse to give into the drive or resentment and you make gold: this is alchemy, or conversion.

Holding in resentment creates a boiling caldron that reaches such a pitch you change man.

Rather than being angry and venting constantly, you hold it in until it transmutes all things.

You wanna get em back, I understand that! But if you don't God'll do it better/knock em flat.

MOSTLY FAKE

God is your Champion and your Avenger. He'll do it much better but not if you declare war.

Forgiving them doesn't mean God won't punish the foe. God's attribute is Justice you know.

Mom said everything evens out in the end. The more I think about this the more I agree friends.

MAKE GOLD ON RESENTMENTS

The more anger and resentment you have the more raw material to make gold then to love.

See the basis of your resentments. Your sins attracted lower companions doing you in since.

Your weakness allowed evil to flow in. Now you're angry--who wouldn't be--at your ruin.

Don't give into a selfie generation of embarrassing self-promotion but work in quiet devotion.

You escaped the narcissist. Now finally you can say what you want and not be harassed.

He controls everything and is the final word. Even his nonverbal indicates you are inferior.

Everything had to be filtered thru him first. My life was in a vice grip, for freedom I thirst.

Hedge of protection: husband won't let enemy in. Hedge down: he opens door to clowns.

Why was the hedge of protection down? Because of YOUR sins: facing this is making gold.

It's all a system. You went crazy, he went crazy that's all. Infinite evil when devil's the default.

MOSTLY FAKE

You have addiction [SIN] and the household falls like dominoes, that's how it always goes.

Hedge down: drunken husband hands wife over to the enemy invading against her boundaries.

SOCIAL DEVICES ARE A TURN OFF

I'm turned off by the social devices I see in you like hideous laughter cackling on a fire.

Why can't you just be real rather than attention-getting and needing approval? It's all inferior.

He knew I needed isolation so the worst abuse he could do was open our doors to them.

Hedge down: drunken husband hands wife over to foe invading boundaries she laid down.

The home, a loving fortress in an evil world, is trashed in a psychological bomb/dark tomb.

Don't shudder at the close calls--God always appears at the last minute and He promised it all.

You bring demons from your addiction [sin] and his own demons come out = trash bin.

Sex sins lead to poverty--of ideation also. The whole ambience of home is degraded ya know.

What was once pure synchronicity and miracles in daily life becomes dark, gloomy, sad--strife.

If you're a dam liar you narcissist everyone knows it. We just go along with it in avoidance.

SEE FOES AS A GIFT

MOSTLY FAKE

See your foes as a gift that keeps giving cuz self-improvement is always your remedy.

The more they hated you the higher your destiny when free. A leader first overcomes the enemy.

By the time a female genius gets to success she's exhausted overcoming social hypnosis.

Social hypnosis: they think what they think cuz the others do just like monkeys who mimic.

Solution: work privately in quiet devotion til completion and The End--your due reward man.

God is not a slaver/pays good wages: justified remuneration and due recognition for artists.

Liberals live in a caregiver's world where criminals aren't dangerous and just need a hug.

To release resentment for good, simply see the system: reactions of hearts of wood to your sins.

The end: you live in a mansion and they're in the streets begging so forgive and go on.

EASY WOMEN

She gave into him cuz she felt something--but he assumed she's easy with every man.

She liked HIM but he doesn't give himself that credit--his sex focus assumes she's a slut.

Most women are logorrheic: diarrhea of the mouth. They tell him all their business right off.

For success you must forgive and if continually bringing up the old scenes, forget it.

MOSTLY FAKE

The end: you live in a mansion and they're still in addiction so forgive em/make millions.

TWO ENDS AND ONE IS VERY BAD

You live in a mansion and they're delirious in a rest home from all their fooling around.

You have renewed youth and beauty like the eagle while they show effects of sins: ugly.

Don't recall when he was a young dashing abuser, see him now: a doddering toothless loser.

For I have broken the teeth of the ungodly: the Lord. He destroyed your foe in this metaphor.

A life of angry unforgiveness shows on the face too. Even believers can uglify, not just a few.

Everything evens out at the end, for there are consequences to purity vs. addiction/sin.

A woman must be disciplined and protected for she'd be used and cast aside if she wasn't.

Once one sees how their sins brought on the catastrophes it's strangely relieving.

Despite repeated problems you wouldn't give up your sins so God removed hedge of protection.

That was why all that crap happened--so stop resentment and put blame on SIN.

SOCIAL MATRIX OR IT'S ILLNESS

You get to a point of uniqueness where you produce or be pegged for mental illness.

MOSTLY FAKE

You don't fit their matrix = you're sick. All tribes and cultures work that way and it's obvious.

Lamentations: Elections are a fraud and the borders are wide open, even people from Yemen.

We've lost our country. Prisons released murderers and they're all coming here--no restrictions.

Thanks alot you democrats/liberal feminists and freaks, you've ruined home and the country.

That's why I'm here behind a locked gate after relocating to a safe place. Do it now ok

Thank you Lord for getting me away, giving me escape. Forgiving those creeps is how I'll repay.

See the necessary resistance of the enemy in building your social muscle then let him go.

No man knows my history. The oldies died/have no memory of it & youth couldn't care less.

For success you must forgive them. It doesn't hurt em you holding a grudge just you, amen.

You're the one who lives in a mansion when all your persecutors are dead, gone or bombed.

Women shouldn't chase men but they ARE so use it as a sifting process/litmus test: NO/not yes.

JESUS WAS SPECIFIC ON HELL

The bible speaks of hell in specific terms: agony, banishment, brimstone, curse, darkness.

Deprivation, destruction, distress, fire, teeth-grinding, guilt, hopelessness, loneliness, pain.

MOSTLY FAKE

Suffering, pressure, prison, punishment, ruin, separation, shame, contempt, smoke.

Sulfur, torment, trouble, trash heap and weeping forever. These were Bible words.

Witch tyrant or benevolent dictator? You're always to blame and she's your loving benefactor.

There are many roads to hell whether a self-righteous religious leader or aid to Adolph Hitler.

Jesus rescues us from the wrath to come. It's a default setting: it's hell or Him in sum.

HOMOSEXUAL SIN: A LITMUS TEST

They don't need us to become activists just desensitize us to homosexual sex acts.

It's not a race or minority needing equality but a perverse sexual behavior disgustingly.

You want us to roll over and play dead in our blind acceptance but we just can't Miss.

Irony of our times: because they perform perverse acts they deserve special rights.

Homosexual sin is a perverse act--nothing more nor less--so don't let sick society normalize it.

When you die you'll find out cuz there's no exit. There's no water, little air, no killing self.

No more hell-fire sermons means millions go to hell having not been told by God's people.

You don't love gays by going along with what they say trying to justify this perversion all day.

MOSTLY FAKE

NORMALIZING PERVERSION

They're normalizing this behavior with five year olds, the quickest way to destroy little souls.

Gays like women as friends? I've never met such gossiping viscous backbiters of our sins.

These perversities are the past after being delivered, washed, sanctified and justified.

Don't forget Christians and church members used to be fornicators, adulterers, swindlers, idolaters.

Conversion therapy implies gays can change--weren't born that way--so they hate it with rage.

Mansell Pattison M.D. was de-chaired from medical school for believing in conversion therapy.

They can't change [born that way] and are even superior gifts to mankind being that way.

They thought they shut us up years back--caved in to flack--but prepare for moral comeback.

It's just like abortion. You'll never settle this issue as if it's dead, blotted out cuz it jumps back up.

The abortion & homosexual issues are litmus tests. Are you a false preacher or true evangelist?

It's easier to be anti-abortion than anti-gay. The latter can get you killed even in your own family.

GAYS AREN'T NICE

Gays aren't that "nice". Hitler's cruel SS guards were sadists and many were sodomists.

MOSTLY FAKE

Lesbians aren't "nice". They're known for alcoholic tirades and domestic violence being pissed.

Don't let liberals dictate this crap because that changes your position with God, your Dad.

They hate/are disgusted with minor sins of women but when it comes to gays they're a champion.

They're just dirty boys on a "fishing trip" and you're saying they're superior? What twits.

You'll get sick of the avoidant relationship: never getting deep, never being listen to, etc.

The crime of our day is seeing homosexuality as a non-sin, a normal and acceptable behavior.

They see it as a fine thing--born that way--not a perversion from which one needs rescue.

LIBERAL ELITES AREN'T NICE

Not only do they say it's normal they demand special treatment from abuse in the past.

They don't need us to be advocates, they just need us not to care. Desensitize to roll over.

This lust is unnatural, twisted and uncontained no matter how much it's glamorized as gay.

Social justice is not only NOT biblical it's a serious hindrance to the true gospel.

Bible says no homosexual or adulterer will inherit the Kingdom of God. You see, it's all bad.

The liberal elite look great, that's part of the game but bible conservatives aren't so vain ok.

MOSTLY FAKE

Liberal elite--majors or comics--look good but are so arrogant you hate em they're so plastic.

Better get involved with politics lest you have inferior men rule over you. PLATO

The defund the police movement is the epitome of the liberal fallacy that man is good, not evil.

The looney leftists blame police for out of control crime in all blue cities not themselves.

If any suburb is nicer than another, it is "racist". Goal: to a common denominator it's all debased.

What do you call a genius in Biden's Homeland Security Dept? A visitor. Sen Kennedy

Biden sees borders as a nuisance and vetting immigrants as racist: we've had it.

Constantly rehashed news but it's about our border so I listen to all the commentaries too.

A WRITER WRITES WITHOUT STOP

The writing is slowing and I'm asking: Lord is this the ending so I can have a holiday finally?

I'm sick of being a relationship coach when so screwed up myself from the early trauma/past.

I would like this to be the words ending but I keep thinking, it even prevents my sleeping.

A few catnaps a day, that's all I can do. One major meal and a snack or two. Music/view

All they did was gossip against me but I was saved from seeing that at the time see.

MOSTLY FAKE

The narcissist is empty so needs approval desperately and doesn't know who he is suddenly.

See your worst abuser as karma for what you were doing including being naive/not knowing.

Caveats: Never confuse narcissistic arrogance with self-esteem, maturity or confidence.

You're living high in a mansion and they're begging in the streets. Forgive/forget those creeps.

Lord make it stop. I no more wanna be an endless spout. I'd like just music/to be off.

Only wordless music is right brained enough for me now, want out from writing compulsion.

TURN OFF THE ENDLESS SPOUT

I'm so sick of writing 18 hours a day for ten years but if that's what you want I'll continue Lord.

When you marry incompetence with ideology it's a disaster every time. Jesse Watters

The only release from the tedious left brain is music and the view so that's what I'll do.

So God saved you and put you in good circumstances. Pay him back by forgiving those dunces.

Even a movie tracks the mind. Only music of the instrumental kind is truly right brained.

I've never met such a self-worshipping clown but no worry they always bring themselves down.

You took us for fools, tried to make it look like ingratitude on our part. Lawyer shysters!

MOSTLY FAKE

A writer writes, a singer sings, a trumpeter trumpets but Lord I'd like to do something else.

I don't wanna be a relationship coach cuz I'm looking forward to being with God the most.

The globalists have brought us down thru SEX. Not until you are married, that is best.

It's the Kalergi Plan: migrant facilities in every town and city, get ready for changes suddenly.

I'm not a relationship coach except to say: "no sex" and "he don't want you". Now you'll be ok.

NO PHONES PLUS FASTING

Dunning-Kruger Effect is when the dumb have control over the elect cuz they don't get it.

They have the power though they're dumber. A helluva situation to. be in but I'm a survivor.

Dad said to hold my head up high lest this happen. Of being misunderstood and put-down.

It's like they own your soul but only if you cave in for no one should control identity you know.

To be misjudged is hell but to play out their script like I did is degradation or death soon now.

Phoning gives em too much opportunity to go off at the mouth. Emails only/tangents-off.

NEVER talk to em on the phone, they'll go off at the mouth. Talk to my agent if you want.

Eat once, snake diet. Eat twice, it's stuck and I wanna die if it doesn't move down darnit.

MOSTLY FAKE

To start Daily Fasting forget WHAT you eat just get in the 22-hour fast habit and eat enough.

As you daily fast your food selections will continuously upgrade naturally/just get into fasting.

I recalled self-recriminating events then God said: the fast will delete all that like an ink blot.

Fasting is a divine lobotomy cleansing and purifying bad memories. It's all fecal matter see.

Comin' to your door soon but they don't care about covid-positive migrants surging through.

RECAP: EMOTIONAL CUTOFF VS. PERSISTENT SYMPTOMS

Queen Consciousness vs. the Average woman. A true emotional cutoff dissolves your symptoms from degrading relationships. If still hooked they will persist cuz it's a system.   It is frightening the bad decisions made to get the other's approval--these inferiors need removal.   If you live for their approval you'll die by their rejection--you're so much happier never thinking about em.

THE KAREN KELLOCK PICTURESTRIP

MOSTLY FAKE

It's mostly fake news and they're tryin' to confuse us. Retreat to self, home, pets/make it all newness.

The whole world is going into tyranny. Even the most neutral countries are coming under scrutiny.

They seek to deconstruct the family--destroy every barrier, you know. Confusion, everything goes.

Canada will now take the children away if the parents don't accept their gender identity--dark days.

Common Core is a shift from teaching facts to attitudes, belief and behavior--it's a failure.

Trump's speeches are at a fourth grade level--simplicity is hard, the function of the bard.

Even if Christian we were messed up by secular humanism and that's why we let em all in.

Black Lives Matter is a terrorist organization and liberals divide us more in a miserable transformation.

Americans are so soft and fragile I worry what's gonna happen to them when it all falls.

Soros is funding these protests and counter-protests. His goal is global control after creating a mess.

America was neat: Can you imagine no need to lock your door at night living right on the street?

MOSTLY FAKE

Reject the brainwash or be more unhappy, choose the vibrant lives of genius sagacity.

God comprehends every detail, the "force" does not.

To adapt to distorted cultural implants men have taken on strange identities.

Woe to those calling evil good and good evil. These are the ones called family/friends and most people.

Jesus came not to unite but divide. He brought a sword to breakup families of the snide.

A man's worst enemies are in his own house. This can be your child, sibling, parent or spouse.

Take the high road by seeing who they are. They got all they wanted but you are the star.

The sick system "frames" us into low self-esteem. They act haughtily but we have God Almighty.

The state and culture puts down marriage while putting up vileness and promiscuity like Cyrus, Miley.

It all started with the hippies, this slide into grossness and going along with the tide of sinfulness.

Little evil creatures, odd looking things: Harry Potter destroyed a whole generation of underlings.

If you sink back into self-delusion over someone, you're no longer on the high road and it's no fun.

MOSTLY FAKE

The popular culture is contrived, plastic, empty, meaningless, retarded and grotesque.

It is tragic releasing sick systems but being relieved of demons outweighs when you missed em.

You just have to take the high road and reject em altogether. They're low: friends of fair weather.

Seeing who they are makes you see who you are--a star--after your relationship had fallen so far.

Why do you wanna hang on to chaos and delay perfection? Don't stop now and think: completion!

They told us how to think, they acted so superior. But God debases the haughty as inferior!

As the years passed mankind became stupider at a frightening rate and the most popular movie was "Ass".

When ugliness is venerated as beauty we know we're in the late stages of civilization: invasive vulgarity.

Water everywhere and not a drop to drink. So much information while people get dumber/can't think.

If we would turn from our wicked ways/repent, God would heal our land and bid foes good riddance.

Movies both reflect and create culture.

Today: Harry Potter creatures, social justice warriors, safe space wimps, angry fascist violence.

MOSTLY FAKE

Not a bunch of books quickly finished but One Good Book that took a lifetime and becomes vintage.

I have tried to explain the liberal mind, how far we've fallen. We've all had trouble from it in someone.

Never force work just think high and it flows out naturally. It's holy spirit ease and makes me happy.

What books are for: to fit historically, to make an amazing dent and that brings fame, obviously.

Don't worry, some will see who you are. Until your time has come you're seen as odd not a star.

Sure you've written a book but will it be read? It implies fame or doesn't fit history as God determined.

You've done the work now it's time to FOCUS on what you want to be: a famous writer, lecturer, trendy.

Great genius always alone. The higher on the bell-shaped curve the more lonely, though on a throne.

All that matters is that you got here, you arrived. Forget the detours and scammers: lessons applied.

It all exists in you--the whole world, all your history, culture, genius too.

And now, nstead of symptoms rolling out triggered by events, your genius rolls out and it's so advanced!

What does it take? Daily assiduity.

MOSTLY FAKE

Solitude: having been brought off from all social rewards I went deep inside, my life was the Lord's.

Human tragedy: with the pure You show yourself pure, with the perverse You show yourself contrary. Psalm 18: 26

God reached down in the sewer to save me and I'll never forget that sewer and the joy of being free.

I just wanna sit and look out the window. It's so pithy with an untracked mind as thoughts flow.

A book isn't like a building where you can see the whole right away--you gotta edit every page.

This is a major work--of course there are changes and tangents.

It's what I do.

It's a career in which I thrive, I very much enjoy and am doing good.

Don't be envious unless you wanna do everything I did to get it.

Courage will fire you up but cowardice will rob you of your soul.

You do not fit the dense archetype so don't worry I'm not talking about you it's just psychiatric.

Every artist needs an agent, if it's your spouse it's best, isn't it.

MOSTLY FAKE

God made the devil who fell. He was beautiful and smart proving anyone can fall, so be careful.

Today's money-making schedule: Sit with music and look out the window.

Never underestimate time alone: looking out the window is such a productive/prolific outflow.

I love husband and he loves me but we both need solitude: bliss for free.

When you go from darkness to light through Jesus, He changes the past to sweet from egregious.

I allow myself to look out the window and up comes precious gems of lucid recall of past events--WOW!

FRENEMIES

Addicts use substances/people to avoid and stays unnourished/hits a void.

Guilt holds us back but after repentance it's usually an implant from other people, don't forget that.

The folie a deux (contagion of madness) gruesome twosome is when the one gives up in exhaustion.

They don't wanna be seen with you cuz the others don't like you. Reject these trendies, eschew.

Old age means you finally don't have to play the game. 70's the new 50: relax into it/ achieve fame.

MOSTLY FAKE

Youth is about boring social but eldering is fascinating solitude with God almighty--wonderful/prolific OH!

Don't view yourself as old or less but soon to heaven/outa this mess.

Old age is not a detriment or disease, it's the icing on the cake after a lifetime of dealing with sleaze.

Eldering/aging is saging. Sagacity brings audacity, what fun: say it boldly when you tell em.

When people fear aging they back into their past. A dusty antique or true maturity: eternal blast.

When I'm in heaven with a brand new body you'll be dying in the tribulation: old, sick and bloody.

Old age: enjoy it, you deserve it. It's the apex of your life not the lowest as youthists like to see it.

The elder was seen as superior in all traditional cultures. It's only inferior with liberal globalist monsters.

I have finally arrived, before I have arrived, by looking at the past not as bad but as a gold mine.

The B.S. of youthist dogmas must be ignored. You're past the argument and agree with the Lord.

I don't need movies but they do jiggle thoughts. All I need is my past, a phantasmagoria that ROX.

MOSTLY FAKE

Old age: enjoy it, you deserve it. It's the apex of your life not the lowest as youthists like to see it.

You like things nice, orderly, clean. Walk away from the rank, the carnal, social, pugnacious or mean.

Have your goal be your own home with a yard, fence and locked gate. Now it's your domain/no hate.

There is nothing more boring than a trendy. Can't you be a little original, and you're not truly friendly.

The trendies are cold, callous and loud. It's cacophony, catastrophe and everything's allowed.

DIETARY ADAPTATIONS

Moving to a higher altitude I had to change my diet. It was fruit or I really felt it and never adapted.

Raw organic dairy made me fat and crazy but with fruit I got energy.

Who needs all that fat in the cells--I'm done with keto forever. Want some fruit, fuel of the clever.

A smoothie fruit base then I use it as an apothecary putting this or that whatever is necessary.

I sip smoothies so I won't be hungry yet I have the best in me.

Cosmic: that's what I feel on fruit. Never felt that on ketogenic carnal fat-fasting and I wasn't cute.

MOSTLY FAKE

Fruit and fasting is joy everlasting as fat dissolves and energy's blasting.

I wanted to eat fat to avoid memories--somehow it distracted from what was painful to me.

Dangerous medical drugs and unnecessary surgery: 2.5 million people every decade die in this tragedy.

250,000 people die yearly from med practices. Journal AMA

Mass deaths are excused by "look at all the good the system does"--huh?

The med profession doesn't fix the bad cuz they're part of the elite wanting to depopulate the planet.

Medical cartel/big pharma is as big as the pentagon but more powerful.

Children and babies destroyed by vaccines.

Every cell was smothered in fat and I couldn't breathe like that.

The major media is covering abuses of the AMA cuz part of their thing is total faith in the system.

Ketosis, fat-adaptation: was on that kick for twenty years tho' miserable and stuck in obstruction.

I never felt cosmic on fat, so oils I avoid or fats from plants.

High Fat: Based on what it did to my body I can say it's a total lie.

Fruitarianism for those worried over aging.

MOSTLY FAKE

My hero and mentor, Arnold Ehret: looked 20 at 50 as a fruitarian/fastarian--it makes you cosmic.

Women should be feline elegant [slim] not chunky muscularity [it's in] but little ladies are a rarity.

Feline slim feminine: only lowfat does that.

Antioxidants, fiber, lowfat: all in the plants.

Don't speak about the glories of dietary fat unless you have flat abs.

Not enough oxygen to heart muscle: attacks don't happen with fruit cuz it opens it up/becomes supple.

Arteries to the heart, ears, eyes, brain--all opens up with fruit in the main.

Diseases from arteries clogged: macular degeneration, vertigo, kidney failure, impotence, hearing loss.

All disease is obstruction through clogged arteries: no oxygen or nutrition gets through, must see this.

On fat I waited for ketosis that never happened (radical health decline) but on fruit it is pure bliss.

It's the FOOD. Smoking and exercise are side issues, scapegoats, platitudes.

The health swamp called Big Pharma is killing millions while enriching those who play the game.

I ate so much butter I felt all the cells were smothered and that made me reverse into fruit forever.

MOSTLY FAKE

Don't let anyone tell you how to do it--that was my problem the first time around but now I intuit.

It was such an awesome thing (spiritualizing the tissues) but I failed when getting involved with others.

When the fruitarian loses his tie to nature he wants noodles, rice and spice but it's not a vice.

It's about fruit and fasting with a starch safety net and it's all ok if salsa and tacos for the day.

Fell off the fruit wagon and took me twenty years to get back. Once you see it, hold onto it as fact.

Gluttarians: Ehret was about frugal fruit--one at a time--and fasting in between, not "all you can eat".

Chinese buffet a sticky spoon joint? That means every spoon, handle and soy sauce jar is sticky, yuk.

The ex-vegan "Nikacado Avocado" says he wants to eat dog. A glutton that has fallen that low?

Some fruitarians got fat because it was a bingefest not frugality and fasting which is how it is blessed.

Ehret said fats cause acid and starches make paste but after detox ok.

Nikakado loves Muslim restaurants and wants to eat dog. Liberals are globalists against God.

The community advancing fruitarian gluttony was tyrannical.

MOSTLY FAKE

Must maintain the thought or lose it: Cherries: cosmic feelings. Bread, pasta, rice: ok but not sublime.

All day smoothies: slim and trim. Cooked starches: ok but wider, puffier, possible constipation.

Cooked starch can be as bad as dairy and meat. Every day I'm more into just fruit/greens/nuts/seeds.

Starch with fat and water-retained spongy tissues: love handles and saddle bags, is this you?

The cooked starch safety net for fruitarians (failed) created a dark force for some, got fat/derailed.

In sensitives, cooked starches turn to paste.

Fruits, greens, nuts and seeds or cooked starch, dairy and meat?

What age and experience teaches you after viewed as a nut: what to eat/not, when to eat/not.

Food: Gotta eat our meal so we have it behind us. No fuss, forget about it now and fast.

Frugal fruit the Ehretian way or massive fruit the Graham way.

Scam: Body positivity is telling women obesity is not unhealthy.

Life is fleeting. Appreciate everything but always trust God, your King.

Diets and restaurants kill. Eat what God moves you to eat with gratitude but watch bad food still.

MOSTLY FAKE

Arrested development of media/Hollywood: childish, peacock, corrupt entitled idiots/we all see this.

This is the greatest witch hunt in political history. Donald Trump

Visceral hatred and unabashed scorn comes through with any mention of him, but I'm unconcerned.

Insane: we'd have to be in war with Russia for it to be treason.

These fake media scam-spoofers look so weird in the face. Even Cooper is no longer an ace.

The democrats put their party politics before everything else and so they lie to you, of course.

The level of mass contagion of madness is astonishing both in the media and in the democrats.

Why are they so afraid of Russia? Why did they hate Sarah Patin? Can't imagine.

Big Pharma is not so much about money but debilitating populations.

Every time one of their scam stories is proven false it points back to them worse than ever: hah!

Brainless media/empty heads can't analyze information, won't even look at it--can you imagine?

Beautiful utopian system of medical care kills 2.2 million every 10 years.

I love fifties movies cuz there's always a moral. I hate modern movies cuz it's an agenda or it's awful.

MOSTLY FAKE

Since the media wears a mask of helping everybody they assume the same of the medical lobby.

Obama and Soros suing Trump and Stone: coming into stuff more ridiculous than we've ever known.

The media's mask of kindness, generosity and loving everybody is to "trust your doctor honey".

They are the ones in bed with the Russians asking for help against Trump: Scam! Scum! Fake stuff!

The democrats along with RINOS/neocons did 100 x what Trump did.

McCain wanted dirt on Trump: "Russian spy".

In my town Obama shut the mines and Hillary sold the uranium, creating devastation/poor bums.

The Obama lawyers are designed to battle with and bring down Trump.

The former president is suing Trump: "I set this up to bring him down".

It's a clash of realities and worldviews.

Watch em become delusional gods like little wimps, as prosperity falls apart cuz they're stuck in sins.

Clueless, moronic behavior by the democrats, more as they let out the rats.

Massive symphony of destruction as the losers become asses, clueless.

Megyn Kelly cratered from ten to 2 million views--she destroyed herself through scams and fake news.

Never interrupt your enemy when they're destroying themselves.

Liberals and migrants are in the cities cuz that's where you get the benefits and make complaints.

Dead cities: Libs get together, die together and will end eating each other.

Get out while you still can: it's all about geographic relocation.

Best friend to minorities is free market and government intrusion is a racket.

Megyn Kelly barely made it going up against Trump but her end was Alex Jones.

Moral relativism says people aren't evil it's their past. If you can't see evil you can't fight against it.

Nine months of accusations with zero evidence of anything illegal.

Sodomism is the ideology of homosexual superiority while seeing hetero Christians as the enemy.

Fake news has always been and millions were killed in the interim: think of that when you hear them.

In history if you didn't tow the line you were ostracized. Now you're a deplorable and despised.

MOSTLY FAKE

Liberals are "pro democracy" and "pro people" but on censorship they are really evil.

Holocaust could never have happened had free speech not been banned--fake news is dangerous man.

Wherever there was no free speech there were massacres. It's happening/fake news triggers.

I'm done with this, the airways are choked with Russia. Tho' a scam that doesn't stop the pressure.

Fake News: They name and shame then forever you're known as a bigot, that's how they do it.

Johnson Amendment: when the clergy went silent in America.

Sure-fire path to an Emmy: come out against Trump.

Pro-war anti-free speech left: Just the opposite of what they were in the past.

It's been around from the beginning: telling lies. That's the fake news we've come to despise.

Love to watch Mayberry on the peaceful sixties before the hippies.

It's good to be anti-establishment cuz it's against Trump and it's adamant.

Trump is our beachhead, we're in the fight of our lives, it's history happening.

Trump doesn't blow his own horn but his accomplishments are America's return.

In this time period the debt was up 600 billion under Barry--we have every reason to be merry!

He turned around economy and ISIS is on the run--do you ever hear of that? No, it's the Russians.

Once the dems felt invincible, but now they're whining, complaining and playing victim.

He's a different breed of cat: not about bragging but turning around the situation, and that is that.

Now we can't "degrade" people in our speech--they determine what that is, it can be anything.

Totalitarians don't want objective rules--it's always them deciding [cruel fools].

Of all churches Baptists and Calvinists the most biblical and they haven't compromised on nuptials.

National debt is down 100 billion dollars after going way up during Obummers.

They think if they betray one of their own, the JCW's will be appeased/not escalate--wrong!

Things get worse, always: appeasement always works that way.

Most don't want harm on others but the left does cuz it silences.

Liberals are no good at debating so they cheat by silencing.

My trophy is minds unlocking. Alex Jones

When globs of sugary niceness didn't work anymore they had identity crisis and that explains this.

MOSTLY FAKE

Liberal niceness worked when victory was guaranteed but when not their anger came out indeed!

I once knew a liberal female who was so nice until that didn't work then she beat on me thrice.

When a device no longer works there's regression to previously successful strategies--adolescent brawling.

Hatred pouring out like green puss after so sugary sweet making a fuss.

Medical Cartel: We love everybody, curing everybody, helping everybody--same as liberal trendies.

So "nice" but when they actually lose they go crazy: so instructive (not nice, underhanded, lying, shady).

These times are the most deceptive since the time of Christ. Everything like what you believe and like.

The IRS controlling preachers through 5013c: Where ever does the gov get off telling us what to preach?

IF 911 buildings were brought down through controlled demolition, it's a much bigger picture to think on.

If you let the government tell you what to preach, shut your doors and go home--a phony and a leach.

God overrules wickedness and deceit and uses it for His own purposes--how neat

If an artifact doesn't support evolution it is dumped in the ocean by Smithsonian.

MOSTLY FAKE

Sick and tired from atheism they'll turn to occult or Satan.

Only he who now letteth will let until he be taken out of the way. 2 Thes 2: 7

Russia scandal mongering is a silver bullet to take out Trump.

Russia-scandaling is a disastrous narrative having long term consequences for the American left.

The Greek humanist model of education is laboratory experience: that's SEX ED and it stinks.

He's the boss--if they don't support his agenda, terminate em!

Homosexuality is the preferred sin of the day and if you say anything against it, it's NOT-OK.

Katy Perry went from singing Amazing Grace to songs encouraging young girls to lesbianism.

First you move into decadence and then into despair. You see this everywhere.

Trump must fire every single Obama appointee to be truly free.

Stars coming from Christian homes then into decadence: within six years it's the dark side or suicide.

To the left, government is their religion and Trump is tearing down their idol into destruction.

What is the government? Clerks and judges and if they're hypnotized, forget it.

They'll be disillusioned with the church: they'll hate the whore. Rev. 17

MOSTLY FAKE

Bio-Ethics: Death panels, deciding who gets care/who stays sick.

Saul Alinksy: The ends justify means, anything is permissible as long as it has our desired end.

They don't practice journalism, they do editorial all the time then wonder why not taken seriously.

Extremist nonsense of the sexual anarchy agenda is becoming law.

The left is evil cuz they don't know God.

Hillary, go away: You keep coming back like you're important--sucking on death and trying to hold on.

10,000 arrests in Wash. D.C. of PBPs: pot-bellied pedophiles.

Only devil worshippers are attracted to children.

Unproductive congress at least blocked the Obama globalist agenda of open borders and taking guns.

The same unproductive congress for 160 years is stopping Trump.

The evil Hydra has nine heads and due to Trump five are already dead.

Bright students rising against anti-Trump teachers with facts and memes.

Admitting how dark it is makes us cherish the light.

The contagion of madness is the spread of evil. It works like any disease as it radically changes people.

Trump is leading civil rights for the unborn. Dr. Alveda King

MOSTLY FAKE

All glossy and insipid, always smiling: That's the new age who loved Obama: silly, wimpy, non-discerning.

Tho' competitive, aggressive and worldly--Trump's brilliant, big-hearted, compassionate and so manly.

Christianity is about the individual not the collective. The schools say to be social, as a directive.

Trump feeds off taking em on, being the underdog: what fun

I just want Mayberry: Andy, Aunt Bee and Opie.

Psychopaths all have a fake niceness about em, like Paul Ryan.

Megyn Kelly we're gonna tear you to pieces when we're done with ya, along with all traitors of America.

Liberals are so stupid they can't see through fakes. If trendies smile they're nice: that's what we hate.

When we're done you'll be seen as the traitor you've always been--make no mistake trash, from your kin.

Pro-humanity, pro-innovation, pro-freedom, pro-free will, pro-wonderment: That's Trump, have your fill.

Wide-eyed wonderment comes naturally with freedom.

You're the pretender: I'll never surrender.

93% of Hillary voters (social justice warriors) live with their parents: floaters!

One person in the right in a sea of lies eventually becomes effective.

MOSTLY FAKE

Gender must be banned because it "restricts choices, aspirations, opportunities"--really?

All glossy and insipid, always smiling: That's the new age who loved Obama: silly, wimpy, non-discerning.

She so makes her presence known I escaped to another room.

Capitalism is: private property and enforcement of contracts. Keep your word and stuff, enjoy life to the max.

Every era will answer for the things it did under social hypnotism in that particular generation.

They act superior cuz they're nice and you're not. You just don't know how cuz genius thinks a lot.

SJW's are ready for catastrophic social change to be "messy, righteous, difficult and necessary".

The country's irredeemably racist so it's SJW's responsibility to destroy it in order to re-establish it?

Hillary can openly commit mass crimes and sell us out but it's Trump who is accused for bad stuff.

He is so evil, he funded Al Qaeda, funded ISIS, caused this crisis but we'll still pray for him I guess.

He funded the massive middle eastern destabilization turning ISIS loose, he quarterbacked the ruse.

He's all about bringing millions of Muslims in, supporting Obamacare and taking our guns.

MOSTLY FAKE

They're banning ads pushing gender stereotypes, which means: women being attractive and sweet.

It's a failed system they can't salvage. That's why congress is blocked, haven't given up on garbage.

We may be losing but winning the ideological war. It's cuz theirs is a failed system we all abhor.

They are too dumb to realize they can't tinker with government medicine only scrap it as mistaken.

Hillary lost cuz she's seen as an authoritarian militant and promoter of war. We're waking up, major.

They're too arrogant to admit defeat by intelligences a hundred times more powerful than theirs.

Enemy hates me cuz I know the info and panicking cuz it's open now.

Let Obamacare fail so we can come up with a great plan instead. Donald Trump

Obamacare wasn't repealed cuz the republican scumbags at the top wanted it--the never Trumper filth.

Even Ron Paul supports Trump: the real deal.

To be a free people we must have privacy.

Every morning there's a new "key detail" to the fabricated plot.

After the Somali killed the nice white lady BLM started celebrating.

Haiti: Hillary kept 99.8%. To the Haitian people she gave .02%

Destroyed: nationalism is something we used to have with pride.

RINOS and NeoCons have good rhetoric (talk) but never deliver.

GOP often yielding to the leftist mob.

Crescendo of politically correct garbage: complementing a female is sexist.

Only 6% of Americans believe the Russian hoax.

They are feeding you an agenda-driven menu.

GLOBALISM AND ISLAM

EU: We don't wanna be in your cool club and neither does Trump.

The globalist in-club roll their eyes over Trump. They're so cool aren't they-- murdering Europe.

The French love Trump cuz they're so sick of invasion by scum.

He doesn't care what they think he only cares about the best interests of the United States.

They replenish dying pops with masses of immigrants, not caring about vulnerable victims.

Globalists are in panic mode making them dangerous and litigious.

They're not "elites" they're criminals: foreign interests above our laws setting up ways to play God.

ABC News: Christians Who Defend Religious Liberty are 'Hate Group'.

Hijab says: You are dirty and shameful to look at so you need to be covered: a walking sin.

Globalists see you as animals, cattle, slaves, fools--using you.

Elites of the world are criminals willing to do bad things so we're digging them out of their hole.

The elites are panicking--getting litigious and ridiculous but that doesn't make em less dangerous.

Islamic rapists don't get prison time, part of the globalist club.

Soros is funding the Obama lawyers.

George Soros who is a foreign Nazi collaborator and destroyed 100 countries is behind all this.

War of Worlds: expect to feel different, dead or jubilant.

Half a million American females had cliteroectomies--are you kidding me?

Russia is Christian again after struggling against communism and that's why they hate them.

Pope Francis is an example of the friendly face of global evil.

North Korea: The Clintons gave em the reactors and missile secrets and Trump's cleaning it up!

ISIS is toast but there are no victory parades cuz he never says he's going in: refreshing isn't it?

MOSTLY FAKE

We're smokin' em out and they know it. Pedophiles too in liberal pockets.

Islam is as dangerous in a man as rabies in a dog. Winston Churchill

Hippies stood for free speech/peace but now they're in control it's silencing/war without cease.

911 was a tool scripted long ago to provide the chaos necessary for the birth of a New World Order.

They wanted to interfere in mankind--do whatever it takes--to create needed chaos, evil snakes.

Luciferians have been seeking one world government for centuries.

The god of bringing all religions together: Lucifer.

Pope Francis is aligning himself against Israel and has declared a Palestinian state, war is near.

98% of Swedish rapes are by Islamicists but blamed on Swedes.

Islam supports pedophilia/enslaving women so the globalists (wanting to overthrow US) love em.

Resist satanic hordes and their pedophile armies: "Lord, please!"

Trump hates the globalist elites and really wants to beat em.

It's the New World Order Pedophile Radical Islamic Base.

The corrupt Vatican, the new world order, the EU, the globalists, Hollywood: all sworn enemies of Trump.

MOSTLY FAKE

Global government is here. If states assert sovereignty they'll confront the EU Navy then the migrant army.

Believe: U.N. and E.U. are setting up a coast guard to bring millions more Jihadis in/not let em leave.

"We must get rid of the white people and their homogeneity". Peter Sutherland, get away from me.

It's one thing to import Muslims cuza low birthrate, but why tell em "keep your culture/don't assimilate".

"We love our Muslims, our Somalis, they're so sweet" after they slit someone's throat in a tweet.

Europe collapsing: Everything mowed down by hordes raping and killing everyone, they are so loving.

Our navy will block your escape and bring our invasion friends in to help dominate you. The E.U.

Tourism UP under Trump, collapses in Europe due to terror/migrant invasion.

Somalia: no government, beyond dystopic road warrior psy-fi films and they want them coming in.

I was waiting for the "dogs are unclean" attacks to start, gonna break my heart.

Tourism up under Trump collapses in Europe down 87%, yep

Why are they sacrificing everything--tourism and sovereignty--to the destructive invading armies?

MOSTLY FAKE

Get this: They wanna bring in African Muslims not Christians--cuz the latter would assimilate easiest?

The new EU coastguard "protects" migrants from the states wanting to block the entry of hate.

They say some European countries aren't being nice enough to the invaders so they block rejectors.

You wanna get outa the EU/never wanted it? We're gonna invade you and block you from fighting it.

The EU is a hostile power over Europe.

Europe's open: free money, housing and women. The AD reads: don't assimilate/do jihad on vermin.

Sexual Jihad: raping women.

If Europe states don't want them EU will block this and bring the migrants in. No Europe, ever again.

It's the EU and UN taking over Europe.

The EU tragedy is authoritarianism, ruthlessness, control, taking sovereignty.

Global elites are dug in and their empire of crony capitalism is back allied with Islam. But it's failing.

We're at a crossroads, there's a vacuum, every person engaged, thank you. The authoritarians are cornered and flailing.

We now see that collectivism is a nightmare scenario and the people who bought into it a fraud, oh yah.

Trump is "insulting to Muslims" so won't be welcomed to the United Kingdom.

The globalists are so insecure they want us dumbed, fat and ugly from what we take in from air/orally.

The elites have turned themselves over and they are beasts.

Elites crushed: You will face the great judgment, be brought low and humbled like everyone else.

Devil worshipping pedophiles: EU, Islamic leaders, pope, Hollywood, Rep-Dem leadership.

They're like gangs who don't assimilate and in response there will be Nazis who don't assimilate.

FOX: Half are hardcore globalist liberals--a peer-pressure cult that cried when we elected Trump.

We're importing absolutely horrific cultures and the fake media won't tell us the truth about it.

Acid attacks every single day, always in Muslim districts so it's all-ok.

Shariah creep has a price too steep. Nip it in the bud/don't go to sleep.

Immigration/diversity is tied to the expansion of state power.

States historically collapsed when faced with balkanization and cultural conflict.

EU stops member nation ships from taken em back to Africa while Soros brings millions in: disastrous.

MOSTLY FAKE

 **Liberals and leftists get raped too cuz they think everyone's good.**

The good man hides himself seeing evil that's coming, the evil man says "it's all good" and is taken.

The EU Master Plan is the complete collapse of civilization.

They're bringing in 80% military age men and letting them do whatever they want and when.

Now they're worshipping gypsies as if their god despite huge crime problems: how odd.

You're now at risk walking your dog because Muslims hate em despite facade.

"I said a Swede raped me so I wouldn't be racist". Oslo rape victim.

Every music concert now has mass rapes. These people are laughing at us, we've made a mistake.

A mob of 1000 migrants attacked a tiny German town's little fair. Imagine the innocent in despair.

There are now stabbings in London every single day. Even open borders liberals are leaving the fray.

Must wear a hood cuz you're raped if not, or acid in the face: Oh God.

Franco-German alliance: Merkron plot 'biggest armament plan imaginable' to make all states pliable.

Dog-walkers: be careful. We have to adapt to their culture, not them adapt to ours and it's awful.

Shariah Creep: Can't show women to be attractive, that's haram and may offend.

MODERN ART FROM HELL
A Social Justice Warrior Smell

REPLACING THE BEAUTY OF THE PAST
BEAUTY AND ORDER REFLECTS HEAVEN
THE ELEVATION OF THE MEDIOCRE
CONSERVATIVES BUILD/LIBERALS TEAR DOWN
PROTEST CULTURE INFILTRATING ALL SECTORS
IDENTITY POLITICS A TERRIBLE THING!
MODERN ART WENT TO HELL
MODERN ART IS FROM THE LEFT
SATAN EXISTS TO KILL AND DESTROY
BLIND LEADING THE BLIND
GLIB TALK BUT INSIDE ROT
CUNNING SINNERS ARE ALWAYS CAUGHT
"DON'T JUDGE" IS FALSE RELIGION
THERE ARE ONLY TWO BIOLOGICAL SEXES DUMMY
YOUTH AN ARMY OF BRAINWASHED BOTS
GIVE UP ON WOMEN CONFORMED OR FAT
MASS DECEPTION OF END TIMES
CENSURE US, WE HAVE BIGGER BACKLASH
INTERNET SALVATION FROM POLITICAL CORRECTNESS
AFTER ENDURING IT, COMING HOME TO ROOST
SWEET LITTLE LADY FROM THE FIFTIES
LEFT DESTROYS ANYTHING ATTRACTIVE
GENDER AND WOMEN'S STUDIES ARE MARXIST
BLACK PANTHER RAISES SELF-ESTEEM
FAT HARRIDANS COMPLAINING OF CAT CALLING
ABSENT FATHER, DOMINANT MOTHER
GOD SEPARATE FROM CREATION: TWO-ISM
HYPNOTIZING COSMOLOGY OF "TRUTH"
DIVERSITY COMES FIRST ABOVE ALL
CONSTITUTION ETERNAL NOT "EVOLVING"

MODERN ART FROM HELL

Modern art is edgy but empty.   It is born of the demented minds of social justice warriors: smelly reality not depth yet with pseudo-intellectual notes they justify this filth.   Modern art is coupled with sophistic explanations--that's ridiculous as it should stand on its own. Before putting too-edgy "art" out there ask yourself: would grandma approve? Modern is uncouth. Through art we sow seeds of discord and that's how societies are taken down by hordes. Europeans are being asked to replace the beauty of the past with the brutality of the present.

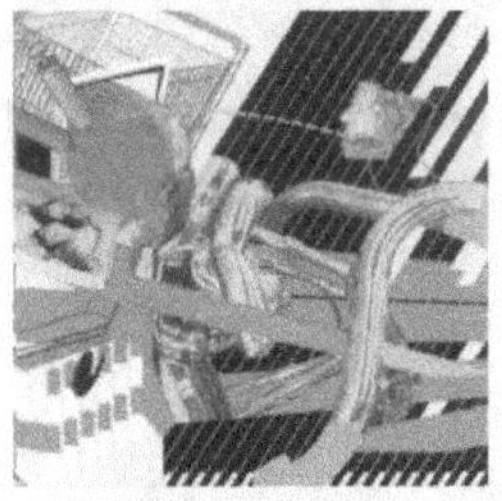

ART SHOULD TEACH NOT DEBASE

Art should be a mediator directing our attention to beauty, goodness, and God in a second.

MLK Statue: From the one end it looks like analingus and from the other holding a big penis.

Artists are under an obligation to awaken our love for beauty. To pull us into God's goodness see.

Ugly art marks a generation. It's sexual, pedophilic, political but art should be a *divine* connection.

MODERN ART FROM HELL
A Social Justice Warrior Smell

Modern art is a physical manifestation born of the demented minds of social justice warriors. Paul Joseph Watson

It's not sensitivity over truth it's moral posturing about sensitivity over truth. Jordan Peterson

Modern art is smelly reality not depth, yet with pseudo-intellectual notes they justify this filth.

Modern art is coupled with sophistic explanations–that's ridiculous as it should stand on its own.

Modern art: edgy but empty.

Before putting too-edgy "art" out there ask yourself: would grandma approve? Modern is uncouth.

Through your art you sow seeds of discord and that's how societies are taken down by hordes.

Europeans are being asked to replace the beauty of the past with the brutality of the present.

REPLACING THE BEAUTY OF THE PAST

Why beauty (the profound/remarkable) matters: without it life's in tatters, there are no answers.

Encroaching artistic fascism of left: only body fluids and self-humiliation remains fair game.

MODERN ART FROM HELL

Just as Puritans were a reaction to filth and debauchery we too became decent, cautious, leery.

Beauty and art is aspirational: it sparks the human spirit to go even higher than we're capable.

There ARE objective beauty standards and it's not a piece of trash in a gallery, it's all backwards.

Beauty is a universal human need elevating the human spirit not ugly buildings as we now have it.

Now we just have nihilism, meaninglessness and unhappiness all reflected in our surroundings.

Surrounded by ugliness we are degraded in our spirit as it drains away capacity for happiness.

The replacement with crap for everything that was wonderful is horrifying to sensitive people.

All "art" is filtered through identity politics before gallery acceptance.

Due to identity politics they shame us into thinking the ugly is beautiful or the hideous is suitable.

BEAUTY AND ORDER REFLECTS HEAVEN

Beauty and order reflects heaven and paradise, ugly disorder reflects hell like the hoarders.

Modern art: obscurantism pushed in pretentious flowery language shaming people to gush over it.

If you don't "jive and resonate" with this crap you're called "uncultured and ignorant" about art.

Are you really serious about this modern art, trying to find the profound and deep meaning? HAH

MODERN ART FROM HELL

Laughing artists never had to study anatomy but can just spatter paint and rake in their money.

Artists are the "sophisticates" who self-delude that it all has meaning to them, the superior beings.

We see trash as trash, but the elevated artist see's the deeper meaning from higher intelligence.

It's all a joke but if they can ascribe meaning to it with pretentious language, they won't go broke.

Dance should stand on it's own, not be encased in pretentious words and meaningless concepts.

Elitism and obscurantism go together: if you can make sense of nothing you're elite or "whatever".

When art has no objective meaning or beauty they rely on obscurantism to dress it up: creepy.

Sometimes their "art" descriptions are three pages long of pure BS and obscurantism, no kiddin'.

Can they let their ridiculous/meaningless art stand on it's own? No, they dress it up, then "oh!"

Trash with a three page description of how meaningful it is and they always get away with it.

If you point out how art is crap despite pretentious words of the hour you're censured and fired.

THE ELEVATION OF THE MEDIOCRE

The elevation of the mediocre to the pinnacle of achievement pulls down the pinnacle in a minute.

To destroy Shakespeare liberals simply elevated crap and then everything fell into their lap.

MODERN ART FROM HELL

Everything traditional like Shakespeare is now being redressed with a "hip twist" which sux.

Art should require talent and skill, not this modern stuff, it's swill.

Pretentious obscurantism surrounding crap art: They do this every time and it's the phoniest part.

If it offends the politically correct it's not art?

You must pass the ideologically purity test to be seen as avant-garde in the modern art world.

Art must reflect the narrative or you're punished as "abusive".

Modern art has become the strange mix of the hyper-real while being utterly devoid of content.

Modern art has become weaponized cuz they control the narrative or overthrow reality instead.

They control the narrative so don't get sucked into premise upon which their "art" is presented.

Modern art closes us from the transcendent while capturing our soul by the cheesy way presented.

The transcendent is beauty and all else degrees of ugliness but we were decent/orderly nevertheless.

CONSERVATIVES BUILD/LIBERALS TEAR DOWN

All thru history it was conservative forces that built civilization and liberals tearing it down.

We should view modern art as a reflection of the final phase of civilization.

Transcendent beauty allows the soul of the viewer to interface with the greater spiritual realm.

MODERN ART FROM HELL

True art raises moral consciousness while organizing understanding of what is healthy/unhealthy.

Poli-subversive art specifically attacks institutions or civic ideas elevating the west above others.

Modern art undermines the philosophical system of an entire group, it's beliefs, customs and values.

Modern art is designed to destroy our historical narrative and the BEAUTY of our spiritual identity.

Modern art uses antithetical elements to disrupt our sense of awe, self-recognition and beauty.

Modern art opens up a moral vacuum where all is meaningless: weaponized against it's own.

Modern art simply politicized anti-art masquerading as virtuous art with genocide it's only arbiter.

Modern art is smelly reality not depth, yet with pseudo-intellectual notes they justify this filth.

Shock art blocks our relation to the transcendent (beauty), we can't relate to ourselves and it's empty.

PROTEST CULTURE INFILTRATING ALL SECTORS

Protest culture is infiltrating all schools as we see mass walkouts and teachers too think they're cool.

You're not artsy if you're edgy, that's the cheap way. True artists create beauty and love decency.

So you're artistic if you adapt to the peanut gallery's debauchery? That's not audacity just nasty.

I didn't think you were that cheap but now I see it's all you peeps: evil offshoots off the main tree.

MODERN ART FROM HELL

I had no idea you were this cheap, evident hater of good, lowdown, cheesy/subversive of decency.

Political art is always subversive of traditions of decency and goodness so how could you trust this?

Stand up comedy's become repetitive cuz it's the same groups targeted--this isn't "edginess".

Artists are petrified of going outa the prescribed boundaries of correctness, producing lousiness.

No one says anything interesting cuz it may taint their careers and boy are they a bunch of bores.

A true avant-garde artist is just himself not a liberal fascist.

Society is degenerating, mental illness is exploding and people don't know God, their Champion.

We've been domesticated and made weak, our families broken up, men and women shallow and dumb.

Identity politics defined: Vote for someone who looks like you, it's easier than thinking too.

When teachers tell kids to walk out it's not "spontaneous uprising" but rather their own agenda/lying.

So if I don't agree with your gun-grabbing agenda I don't care about kids? Watch this sly fib by libs.

The kids refuse to sit in classrooms with armed teachers, they want to punish us all in the suburbs.

They say all masculinity is bad, oppressing women--not that we need men to keep out the vermin.

IDENTITY POLITICS A TERRIBLE THING!

MODERN ART FROM HELL

Identity politics is a terrible thing, setting us against each other--it's Satan not our Christian brothers.

Identity politics is pure tribalism and playing that game is murderous like with white Africans.

Learn to proceed despite your "victimization status" and be normal everyday chumps like us.

Old white males are the main targets however they are given the lowest victimization status.

Virtue signaling is being politically correct to get approval and an immature trait needing removal.

Modern art is a physical manifestation born of the demented minds of social justice warriors. Paul Joseph Watson

Cleaning lady threw away expensive modern art she mistook for trash.

MODERN ART WENT TO HELL

Cleaning lady threw away expensive modern art she mistook for trash.

Modern art: edgy but empty

Are you really serious about this modern art, trying to find the profound and deep meaning? HAH

Modern art: obscurantism pushed in pretentious flowery language shaming people to gush over it.

You must pass the ideologically purity test to be seen as avant-garde in the modern art world.

Art must reflect the narrative or you're punished as "abusive".

Modern art has become the strange mix of the hyper-real while being utterly devoid of content.

MODERN ART FROM HELL

Modern art has become weaponized cuz they control the narrative or overthrow reality instead.

Modern art closes us from the transcendent while capturing our soul by the cheesy way presented.

We should view modern art as a reflection of the final phase of civilization.

Modern art undermines the philosophical system of an entire group, it's beliefs, customs and values.

Modern art is designed to destroy our historical narrative and the BEAUTY of our spiritual identity.

Modern art uses antithetical elements to disrupt our sense of awe, self-recognition and beauty.

Modern art opens up a moral vacuum where all is meaningless: weaponized against it's own.

Modern art simply politicized anti-art masquerading as virtuous art with genocide it's only arbiter.

MODERN ART IS FROM THE LEFT

Any teachers who are left are survivors of the hard-left indoctrination environment and the worst.

The replacement of facts and analysis with political hysteria and abuse: that's the public schools.

They don't want diversity at all, they only want a fascism of feelings. Stefan Molyneux

Politics: Not facts but people controlling hysteria by lashing out at opponents in America.

Intergenerational sex (pederasty) is bad. Milo said it was good so he's dead.

If your art is political it's ok when they're in control but later the backlash will be harsh and bold.

MODERN ART FROM HELL

Getting rid of 60's shows like Mayberry wasn't a rural purge it was a white purge/now it's city sludge.

Being open to their flattery is a serious weakness so you'd better get tough or it's over for us.

Do not greet nor receive false teachers into your house or you participate in their evil deeds. John 2

They wanna punish the whole country cuza what some lunatic did--that's the kids.

This generation is so off-base it's a turkey shoot, a cakewalk to correct their fallacy with your talk.

It's like an evil tidal wave as false doctrine (one-ism) takes over everything but it's a lie: nothing.

I was a terrible filthy sinner but God turned it all around, forgot it all and made me a real winner.

Each of the 30,000 Christian denominations say they are the only way but it's just Jesus I say.

SATAN EXISTS TO KILL AND DESTROY

Satan exists to steal, kill and destroy. How does he do this? Through false doctrines minimizing this guy.

The bible raises man up from slavery and degradation, then they become useful citizens again.

A sermon is only based on the fruit it bares, so ignore all those golden-tongued orators.

Bible tries to get man to face his sins and repent for them, because Jesus' sacrifice *erased* them.

Many words--volubleness or loquacity--marks the false doctrine. Truth may be said in few words quickly.

Look at the *fruits* of religion: we were rich and influential when we were a Christian nation.

The youth don't know, so they pump em full of garbage trying to destroy their mind/keep em below.

If a man walked into a lady's bathroom he woulda been crushed by real men angry/furious too.

BLIND LEADING THE BLIND

Your teachers don't have a clue.

If you're a preacher God has anointed you already but what happens when the crowd gets angry?

Saying some crazy hippy spouting lies is your guardian angel? This is crazy and unbelievable!

Churches have fallen into lies, fables and disrepute! It's all from carnality, compromise/no fruits.

Seems you serve a small God not big One, and you accept other religions as equal = mockery and sin.

Christians differ on things like baptism etc. but they all agree He died for you/me--that was America.

Everything has it's meaning and identity in Him, He created the universe and everything therein.

God has chosen the foolishness of preaching to save them that believe so He sets them apart, see?

Yes! We divide because we hate sin and everything else that HE hates, as he instructs us each day.

It's happened to boys/girls: turned from Jesus to ignorance, paganism and darkness of that world.

MODERN ART FROM HELL

People seek joy through religions of works, not realizing it was already done at the cross first.

At war with relatives and maniacs: All over the world they're turning from the truth of God to a lie.

GLIB TALK BUT INSIDE ROT

Glib talk but inside rot, perversion and destruction--a buffoon and fraud and you knew it not?

Hah--a man who worshipped his own mind, and his brain! He'll be mowed down like the grass I say.

There are laws so there must be a law-Giver.

Hell is at the end of a Christ-rejecting life.

A false preacher says nothing about the cross--nothing! Also not sin or it's remedy, how wanting.

Man's problem is not lack of intellect but a fallen nature--his heart--which "niceness" covers in part.

False healers think they can educate you out of problems, never mentioning sin and the fallen.

Education is not the answer, only salvation is the answer and that comes from a Person.

College professors going to hell talking like that--like Savior means nothing or occult is a good thing.

My pain is greater than I can bare said the sinner.

Entire congregations go apostate preaching liberalism like pro-sodomite or pro-abortion!

You only care about trendy things cuz you're part of this world and it's unlimited debaucheries.

If your church is that way it's not God but man-made--get out, escape and let Jesus save the day.

The violent hatred towards Christianity is growing daily so preach it I say.

He felt bad about what he did but not enough that Godly sorrow would worketh repentance.

CUNNING SINNERS ARE ALWAYS CAUGHT

Cunning sinners are always caught--God laughs at the slobs.

Do you worship people--status or stars? Watch as the worms eat them and they disappear.

Even his nation's worst enemies hated him for treacherously selling out his own country.

They're gonna false flag it and blame it on us--that's what they do and we all know it.

Staged terror is part of our vernacular cuz we made it popular as truth-lovers.

If we can no longer debate and present our sides then it's tyranny and violence besides.

It's no longer easy preaching the bible as the final authority cuz they think THEY are the authority.

They're hauling pastors off to prison for hate speech, for not bowing to government to deceive.

The left is successful at making simple facts seem rude, evil and unkind.

Gun control persists: Enlarging the state and disempowering citizens is in the left's best interests.

Mexico bans guns and has the highest crime rate in the world.

They yell "do something--not one more child". Not a word about Islamacists killing millions--why?

MODERN ART FROM HELL

To prevent mass killings stop drugging our young boys. Alex Jones

A fetus is sentient, feminists!

Trannies degrade our fighting capabilities and make war in the barracks. Any idiot can see this.

Whenever someone says "don't judge" it's them judging YOU. Don't EVER be talked down to!

Judge: Make your own determination of reality, not adapt to "superiors" who censure but are petty.

"DON'T JUDGE" IS FALSE RELIGION

The "don't judge" myth is either public schools or false religion so judge and don't be chicken.

Psalms starts out with hicks trying to bring down kings. They assemble to plan their evil stings.

Mexico: Total gun ban for citizens, highest crime rate in the world yet you go along with this?

Be merciful to me O God, for man would trample or devour me: all day long he oppresses me. Psalms 56: 1

"Be liberal, let us take over, we'll be sweet" then they conquer and kill and they're the same still.

Not born that way: Women are dumbed cuz they want each other's approval more than truth, ok?

They lie in wait for me/would swallow me up or trample me all day long, and there are many. Psalm 56: 2

Is Trump out of joint? The constitution remains the same no matter who's in power--that's the point.

MODERN ART FROM HELL

How the sexes get along is the basis for society but now "he" can beat her up in wrestling, really?

We're now required to lie about biology/punished if we don't. Reason's gone/hearts of stone.

Soon it will be illegal to even teach biology to accommodate the latest liberal cosmology.

How insane a celebrity's profuse apology for mis-gendering nut jobs in this new pathology.

Ruining a girl's state championship for all the undrugged, unsteroided aspirants who haven't flipped.

If you wanna be a girl or boy, do it: take up violin not wreck a sport for all the other participants.

THERE ARE ONLY TWO BIOLOGICAL SEXES DUMMY

There is no gender fluidity--there are two biological sexes, dummy.

Ban baseball bats, knives, screwdrivers, cars. They're used in crimes too so change all the laws.

It's Germany in 1933: they confiscated guns, eliminated free speech and censured the media.

Fill people with psychotropic drugs with "mass killing" on the insert then say it's the guns": jerks.

L.A. has become unrecognizable. In reaction white flight escalates as they turn red states blue.

Governments never give you back what they've taken away, so give the left no quarter, ok?

Why would we possibly need AR-15s? Because the enemy has AR-15s, see?

A reprobate mind is conditioned not to know evil and insists we do things that are inconvenient.

MODERN ART FROM HELL

The left is never, ever satisfied. They will take everyone's rights then turn on their own kind.

Once they get rich they want power which is intoxicating. More and more the left is conquering.

The unified religion is Lucifer.

They seek satan after told they'll feel a wonderful strength, energy, lightness and rapture.

The gun agenda is only a tactic in the goal of total control and that is what every good patriot knows.

They probe in little attacks so later when the main attack happens we don't recognize it.

YOUTH AN ARMY OF BRAINWASHED BOTS

Youth are an army of brainwashed bots who take the latest political correctness and bully us a lot.

First they censure then demonize, arrest then kill--and they're cutting off our money and speech still.

Choose your side but we'll win regardless.

Stay level headed, stay strong. Because they're gonna come in to get you or pull you down.

It's our second amendment right. We need better guns than our enemies, invading mobs or armies.

Don't budge one inch when it comes to the left. Don't thrown them a bone because it's like theft.

If your enemy has a sword, get a better sword.

Old lady defends against mobs and thugs. Guns are the equalizer and Trump's betraying us.

Women are shallow and stupid cuz they love The View, Joy Behar and are hypnotized by each other.

Voting is more dangerous than guns--what if a million teens voted in a thug?

Women are stupid, shallow and cruel because they listen to Joy Behar, Whoopi and The View.

Women love to assert their authority thru gossiping/networking and how I hate it.

Virtue signaling defined: Taking the politically correct view on a trendy topic to not seem unkind.

Conservative patriotic husbands of liberal wives cannot get thru to them so see that/do not despise.

GIVE UP ON WOMEN CONFORMED OR FAT

It's hard to give up on all women but you just about have to do that, they're just too conformed or fat.

I love God and hate liberalism so I guess that is my contribution to the failing nation.

Christianity is not a set of rules but God/a Man who saves us from the whole mess or fools.

Occult is in all Disney movies: hexes, incantations, sorcery, spells, curses-- also seen in churches.

Tarot, astrology: With all the time you study occult you ignore Jesus--you're not Christian just a nut.

Disney's plan: Instill occult curiosity, elevate animals and dehumanize humans, basically.

Disney's magical world of witchcraft seduced us as kids and now we're paying for it, ya dig?

MODERN ART FROM HELL

Fascinated and snagged by tarot cards she also gets bitchy and fallen cuz that's how it works.

The very things they say they hate their movies are full of. They want guns while you've none of.

Our founders gave us a great trust fund--not gold but the right to self-defend.

Wise as a serpent--we're not supposed to be stupid and God doesn't like it.

Book of Job or Book of Joel Osteen?

Mass deception of the end times is unfolding now.

MASS DECEPTION OF END TIMES

Gun control is always, without exception, followed by storm troopers and a dictatorship.

Their ratings went from super low to in the tank so of course Joy Behar et. al. are walking it all back.

Their plan is to weaponize the third world and then use it to reverse-colonize the first world.

How to bring the west down: Celebrate and glamorize the beta male or call men clowns.

It's not a sign of love to go along with their B.S. just because they virtue signal as feminists.

Not only will they reject you for your political views they'll fire, gossip, ruin, and slander you.

The archetype of the older white Christian family man is racist and it's an insult and false.

History of the 20th century: giving up what worked for what sounded nice.

It is our God-given right to defend ourselves against lunatic mobs invading our house.

MODERN ART FROM HELL

The constitution says THIS--it's not up for debate. But the left can't debate anyway, they run away.

Since the conservative deals in rational, logical arguments the left can never win a debate and exits.

The left is so boring and shallow, always virtue signaling on trendy topics based on hell below.

The left's only argument with logic and reason is: I just don't like it so I'll accuse you of racism.

Go ahead and make your art political--you're in the wrong and soon they'll all see it, get me gal?

Go ahead and block, ban, purge and censure: the populist movement will grow beyond measure.

CENSURE US, WE HAVE BIGGER BACKLASH

Generally we just wanna be left alone but if you keep forcing us to agree there's gonna be fallout, see?

Calvinists start on time they don't wait for the last stragglers dragging in, adapting to decline/SIN.

You're so dumb and shallow you'll accept any line to tow but you'll switch just as fast ya know.

You'll accept any crap (not having your own map) and then virtue-signal to the crowd of cads.

The only way you'd ever see reason is if the other's committed treason to that view, appeasin'.

In a war you recognize the enemy as evil, period. You don't sit and argue his pros and cons, get real!

"Call me by your name" glamorized pederasty and how disgusting for boys, a terrible tragedy.

MODERN ART FROM HELL

Study: All growing churches are conservative, all declining churches are liberal, no exceptions.

They threw away orthodox Christianity and adopted the secularist globalism we call church today.

The whore church like Methodists are losing hundreds of thousands a year: apostates and queers.

The false church never preaches sin and repentance if that goes against the party line perchance.

Theological conservatism is the key to congregational growth, without exception.

Conservative Christians growing and maintaining faith multigenerationally but libs aren't having babies.

Libs are the voice of the "excluded and marginalized" so the white man is the class to despise.

INTERNET SALVATION FROM POLITICAL CORRECTNESS

The great mass blowback against political correctness found it's home online.

They want us like Brazil: Guns in hands of cops and criminals while we're caught in the middle.

Your interest in them is tantamount to people-worship so stop it.

Societies are rich because the people there are intelligent with an aptitude to make things work.

Public schools are government schools to sell you the current narrative and thus you're not intelligent.

When thugs invade your house remember to be inclusive and show em where the refrigerator is.

The hated racist is "alienated by the other".

MODERN ART FROM HELL

According to Pelosi we oughta thank the Dreamers and the parents cuz they're better than us.

Watch out for the kids who say free speech is the same as racism. Yes, it's gone that far ma'am.

Watch out for somebody who says they love everybody cuz either they're lying or their crazy.

According to UC saying you're not racist means you're racist--it's a micro-aggression they insist.

The Puritans (which I am) were into austere order and solemnity (no chattering or jocularity).

The Puritans got that way as an adaptation/reaction to the debaucheries of 18th century England.

AFTER ENDURING IT, COMING HOME TO ROOST

We've endured treachery, deceit, laxness/laziness so now we're reversing to the other extreme.

Our youth are disordered from programming. We're sick of this crap and want a return to reality.

We know the exact signs of liberalism and will respond, in kind, every time but we'll stay refined.

Mega-churches are swinging clubs.

Clinton opposed gay marriage for decades until she hopped on the train to win the progressives.

That's the way women are: getting the approval of each other supersedes truth-seeking, wow.

Destroy us by making us lackluster--no culture, not even gender, conformity to the master.

They aren't partisan views, they're get-even views. Alan Dershowitz

MODERN ART FROM HELL

Women have never been so well treated as by western men yet you're conflating like they're all hellions.

Feminism has become a joke and high-paid power women are distancing themselves, unyoked.

If your "art" is political you'll be so embarrassed later (eat crow when things change): disfavor.

You've been taught bunk in the schools, ball-faced lies. Do your art around it and be despised.

Don't talk em out of it just let em do themselves in. Evil brings itself down in family or friends.

They're personally unattractive cuz that is giving in to patriarchy but this is deceptive malarkey.

SWEET LITTLE LADY FROM THE FIFTIES

Be a sweet little decent lady from the fifties--now you'll have power, not thru roles or filled with sin.

Feminism makes men enemy, wimped and cuckolded or an instant adversary sensing treachery.

Feminists deny hating men but what about ruining the boy scouts? The list goes on, feminism sux.

A boob job doesn't give you power, many get even bigger boobs and it all goes down from there.

Before the grossification of culture men preferred elegance: tiny boobs, slimness, niceness.

Think about it: it's absolutely sick this boob job thing--how insane these caricatured dames.

The boobjob dame may also be into occult: tarot cards etc. cuz it all goes together in America.

Men should return to reality and actually feel fear of boob jobs/sex dolls, fake reality not the rose.

She can decide later it was rape and you're toast--destroyed. Get her to sign it or it's best to avoid.

What if three years from now she takes a radical feminist course and decides it was rape?

No need for signs of violence/she can chase him for weeks--his life is still destroyed as she speaks.

The very essence of civilization is that men will sacrifice themselves to save the women.

LEFT DESTROYS ANYTHING ATTRACTIVE

Left destroys everything attractive in favor of the bland, the mediocre and the dysfunctional.

Political correctness is a war on noticing. Steve Sailer

Gender/women's studies are thinly-veiled leftist propaganda vehicles not academic disciplines.

Never argue with the idiots who bring you down to their level and beat you with their "experiences".

Being drawn into heated arguments is fruitless and exhausting so we stand idle and in denial.

Having lost ability to think they can hold two contradictory premises in their head without a blink.

Like rust, the radical leftist corrosive presence in our midst never sleeps, so either can we.

If there is no brown in the rainbow it must be racist and corrected (against natural order as God did).

MODERN ART FROM HELL

If you don't play by their rules you are quickly and viciously ostracized as stupid bigots and fools.

Everything must change without reason or logic as constantly shifting boundaries destroys societies.

Constantly changing the left keeps us vigilant as to what is acceptable behavior and what is not.

The left keeps it's brutal power thus: by embarrassing and scaring everyone into silence.

Only strict obedience to the anti-logic of the left will do.

We can't dialogue with the left using it's concepts and language lest our own viewpoint changes.

GENDER AND WOMEN'S STUDIES ARE MARXIST

Gender and women's studies based on cultural Marxism are inherently non-academic disciplines.

Communist takeover so hidden under obscure texts or curriculum we just couldn't see em.

Communist takeover was shady, hidden under unlikely curriculum titles like "American Studies".

While we snoozed they stole our defensive weaponry--allegiance to the constitution/being free.

Always tell em their war is for "freedom" and "democracy" yet no speech or opinion you see.

Weaponized cloudy philosophy into ideological anthrax ready to deploy at a moment's notice.

Radical environmentalism, artistic communism, psych-analysis of opponents = multiculturalism.

MODERN ART FROM HELL

Left came up with "repressive tolerance" (for everyone but us), also known as political correctness.

Embarrassed for sex (that's you later) when you wake up to degradation of public schools, a mess.

Their goal is to shut down speech making us vassals and malleable, fearful of their punishment.

Make us so confused, timid and apprehensive of punishment we become basket cases not patriots.

Boob jobs and tarot cards.

BLACK PANTHER RAISES SELF-ESTEEM

Black Panther will be in school curriculums as reparations teaching white children what they ruined.

Panther raises black self esteem but also pathological sense of grievance against white people.

They've been given an attractive myth as honorary citizens of Wakanda not oppressed in America.

As they have fantasies of power and success we are to feel shame and guilt for creating that mess.

We are to feel shame and guilt for the deeds our ancestors actually accomplished--think of that.

What's making you sick: victim ideology politics.

History is there to take us off the train tracks of ignorant inevitability and restore our will freely.

Trump's gonna decriminalize pot: reining in Sessions and making him hot!

The loving left is always calling for WAR, in a reversal like we've never seen from long before.

MODERN ART FROM HELL

Feminists letting themselves go because to look good would please men--patriarchy--their foe.

Feminists accept their fat because they have a right to be anything they want even that.

Are men really catcalling these unattractive, fat, mannish harridans, the feminists? Oh come on....

Men used to catcall sweet young ladies and it was flattering but now it's called "disempowering".

FAT HARRIDANS COMPLAINING OF CAT CALLING

How funny a fat harridan complaining about catcalling--the feminists are falsely accusing!

Why should they take a bath, why should they do anything? Pleasing to men? that would be giving in.

Why should she lose weight for him? She'll gain more and end up alone or with cats she adores.

Majority of American females wanna create a home for husband and kids, anathema to feminists.

New feminists look like they smell, and smell like they look but with sweet little ladies it's all it took.

Old feminists purposely look like old hags with blue hair. A lady is pleasing at any age, not a scare.

Her new feminist friends will be a dark spirit invading the household and you'll feel the cold.

Worse thing is: sick feminists know nothing about politics but get in their licks and have influence.

The new feminist wants to be "famous and rich, not that crazy bitch" cuz it's divisive/leftist.

MODERN ART FROM HELL

Let the feminist in and soon you'll see tarot cards, Harry Potter books even lesbian stuff--yuk!

Feminists are not for women but getting attention and mimicking all they hear from vermin.

ABSENT FATHER, DOMINANT MOTHER

Absent father, dominant mother = Jezebel spirit: don't bother.

A man can only love a woman if he respects her so stop demanding it and act right for it.

How can he respect you if you follow the feminist crowd of fats, acting like that, spewing crap?

Ha ha you complaining about male cat calls--are you kidding, you expect us to believe you all?

A woman who looks nice for a man (dressing for him) is a "sell out, man"--that's the feminist scam.

The California bay area liberal elite groupthink wants to ban the holy bible and make it illegal.

In this deep state mess, espionage is a science, propaganda an art and sabotage is a business.

Libtards think gun free zones stop mass shootings--nothing proves more they're a mental illness.

Tyrants in history felt invincible but when people woke up they were thrown into graves, humbled.

Cosmology of the bible is separation. Father is separate from children: he punishes but blesses again.

The confrontation is between two world views.

The only solution to modern misery is the biblical worldview of God vs. creation.

Twoism: We have the wisdom of God as a totally separate being from the things He made.

GOD SEPARATE FROM CREATION: TWO-ISM

The most profound truth of this generation: God is separate from His creation.

What is made must be two, not one.

Oneism is an all-inclusive self-justifying cosmology: "personal empowerment" and "human flourishing".

Oneism completely leaves God out. Not individual empowerment but repentance than God's blessings on man: awed.

No longer called "new age" they just say "I'm spiritual but not religious".

Oneism is "a theory about everything".

Oneism understood: any notion of sexual morality must go, all sex is good.

Oneism comes over youth as a totalitarian coherent system. Oneism is all bull—"not two"—its just Hinduism.

Twoism is the key to the cosmos everywhere but especially sexuality.

Young people's questions are not answered, for example about transgenders. It's not in the bible but just paganism.

Born this way--an original sin DNA? Accept but don't approve, for homosexuality results from the fall, ok?

HYPNOTIZING COSMOLOGY OF "TRUTH"

Their self-identifications make no biblical sense. If you buy into it you'll never get to your next place and stay dense.

Cure for the mentally sick: a deeply bible-saturated apologetics.

Non-gender clothing: "pure expression of self".

The only answer to a self-justifying all-inclusive cosmology based on the lie of oneism is the Truth.

Paganism in the elites produces degraded results in the race. The oneist is overwhelmed by self-will, dis-grace.

The wise are intimidated by all-is-one politically correct thinking so the church is degrading.

Give em the tools to analyze what's happening in the church, to use twoism the solution that works.

Our universities have abandoned all reason to be politically correct--can you imagine that?

University says: Ideas should not be debated, but repressed and the True Self never expressed.

The Clintons have turned the politics of personal enrichment into an art form for themselves. Trump

DIVERSITY COMES FIRST ABOVE ALL

Willfully and eagerly sacrificing everything on the altar of "diversity" and "inclusion": this is confusion.

Trump knows how to show power and no one else does. it can't be faked: it's innate in the high crust.

If these social justice warriors take over we'll be dragged from our homes at night: a blight.

One wonders if he'll have enough time to turn it all around. The devil's working so fast, a siren sound.

With liberals in control it's an upside-down universe. Cronies aren't punished while we are cursed.

With liberals in control we put up with so much crap. Every day it's a new shoe to drop, a new map.

MODERN ART FROM HELL

Why do liberal cities become stinking fetid rat holes? Crime/scams, you know.

Extremism in defense of liberty is no vice. Barry Goldwater

Freedom only comes from the clenched fist of truth. NRA

California's soft-on-crime mentality made us a victim and it's the same in all liberal cities and towns.

The left wants to suicide the country cuz they want Cloward and Piven [they don't want prosperity].

They wanna wreck it all to rebuild it but it never happens that way as they sink in their swill/ruin it.

CONSTITUTION ETERNAL NOT "EVOLVING"

Democrats look at the constitution as evolving through time while to Reps it's eternal foundation sublime.

We are non-suicidal, non-nihilist, common sense constitutionalists.

All logic is gone, now everything's by rote: Stuff they've contrived while they boast.

With liberals in control there is no justice. As God's main attribute, of course this disgusts us.

Did they purposely not do a good job for you cuz you're conservative? Please think about this.

Why did they distress us? Because they were liberals of course.

THE HERD IN WORDS
HIX POLITIX
HOW THEY RUINED US
JUST SKIP DINNER
LE FEMME AND THE COMMUNIST SPIRIT
LIBERAL CHAOS & ROT
LIBERAL DOUBLETHINK
LIBERAL GALL 1 & 2
LIBERAL SHOVE-DOWNS
LOCK YOUR GATE
MANUAL FOR SUPERIOR MEN
MODERN ART FROM HELL
MOSTLY FAKE
NOTES TO CHAMPS 1 & 2
OVERCOME FRENEMIES
PC MAKES US CRAZY
PEOPLE ARE CRUEL
PEOPLE PROBLEMS 1 & 2
PERSECUTED GENIUIS
POLI-PSYCH MYSTERIES
PRETENTIOUS SLOBS
QUEEN BEE
RETURNING TO FIRST NATURE
THE SCHOOLS SCREWED EM UP
SEASON OF TREASON
SEPARATE MEANS HOLY
SOCIAL HYPNOTISM
SOLITUDE SOLUTION
SUPERCILIOUS
TOAD TO PRINCE
TRIALS CYCLES
TRUMP VS. GROUP
TRUST IN TRASH
THE TRUTH ABOUT PEOPLE
UNDERHEANDEDLY CLEVER
WALK TALL WITHIN WALLS
WE'RE NOT ALL ONE
WINNERS SKIP DINNER
WORK OR SMERK

AUTHOR BIO
Karen Kellock Ph.D.

Ph.D Political Psychology, UCI 1976
Post-Doctoral: UCI Medical School
Department of Psychiatry
Grants NIMH, NIAAA

Ph.D. dissertation "A Systems-Theoretic View of Pathologic Interaction" made an early mark as the "Wife of the Alcoholic Syndrome". Postdoctoral research at UCI Medical, Dept. of Psychiatry on the systems surrounding pathology on NIMH and NIAAA federal grants: The Contagion of Madness: The Psychology of Neurotic Interaction and Pathological Systems. Therapy tool Therapeutic Playwriting introduced the play Mary and Murv: Gruesome Twosomes in the Alcoholic Marriage. She taught Abnormal Psychology and Pathological Systems Theory at UC and CSU campuses and developed "the Debris Theory of Disease" in 100 books and website: (www.karenkellock.org).